Travelling to a Holiday by the Sea

COLOURED VERSION
CHILDREN SAVING OUR PLANET SERIES

CAROL SUTTERS

Illustrated by William Fong

AuthorHouse™ UK
1663 Liberty Drive
Bloomington, IN 47403 USA
www.authorhouse.co.uk
UK TFN: 0800 0148641 (Toll Free inside the UK)
UK Local: 02036 956322 (+44 20 3695 6322 from outside the UK)

Because of the dynamic nature of the Internet, any web addresses or links contained in this book may have changed since publication and may no longer be valid. The views expressed in this work are solely those of the author and do not necessarily reflect the views of the publisher, and the publisher hereby disclaims any responsibility for them.

This book is printed on acid-free paper.

ISBN: 978-1-6655-8642-9 (sc)
ISBN: 978-1-6655-8643-6 (e)

Library of Congress Control Number: 2021903665

Print information available on the last page.

Published by AuthorHouse 04/15/2021

authorHOUSE®

Our Holiday train journey

School has just finished and it is time for the family summer holiday. Mum spoke, *"We will not travel by aeroplane to Scotland this year but by train as we want to reduce our carbon footprint and cause less pollution."*

The family embarked on a train journey to Scotland to see their grandparents.

As Kate looks out of the window she sees some tall windmill like things in the distance.

"What are those?" asks Kate.

"Those are wind turbines," replies mum.

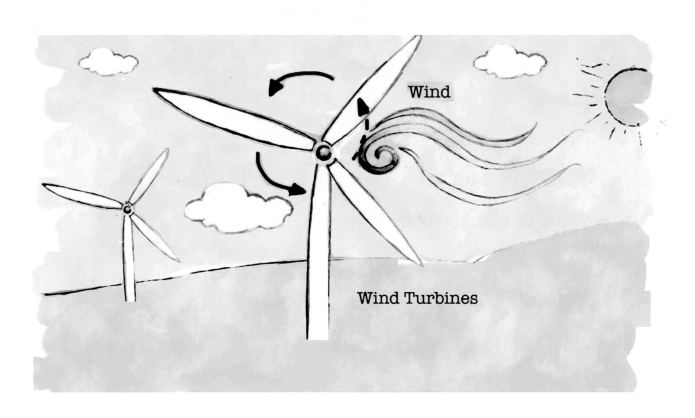

Wind

Wind Turbines

"Wind turbines can be used to make green energy. This does not use fossil fuels from the ground or sea as an energy source. The force of the wind turns the fans on the wind turbines.

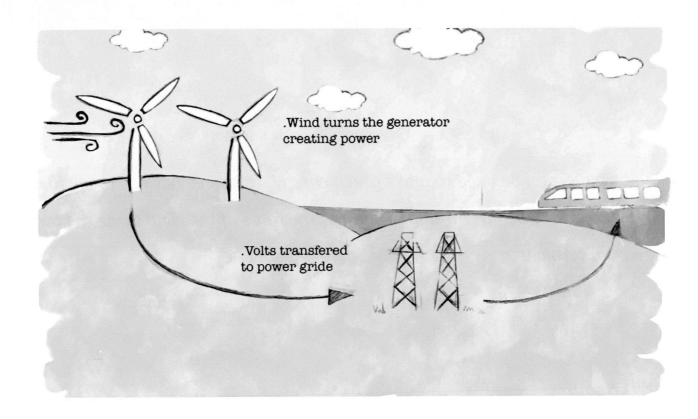

.Wind turns the generator creating power

.Volts transfered to power gride

This is a natural source of energy. The rotating fans transfer their energy back to the Power Grid at the Electricity Station and this electricity can be used to power trains. Wind turbines can also be found off shore. This is part of our approach to reduce carbon emissions. If we use renewable energy sources, we reduce the use of fossil fuels and so cause less pollution."

Mum suggests, *"We will discuss the carbon energy we used to go on holiday on our return home. This is called our carbon footprint."*

"From the Electricity Power station it also comes to us at home," says Tom. *"Yes that is correct,"* says Mum. *"Very well remembered."*

Kate decides to draw a picture of a wind turbine to take to her grandmother and to show her friends when she returns to school after the holidays.

As the train passed the next field the land was covered with grass. *"This is what we are used to seeing in the countryside,"* mutters Mum. *"Fields with cows grazing on the grass."*

The cow in the field utters a big "Moooo" as the train speeds past.

"But now there are new types of farms as we can see ahead. A solar farm."

"There are so many fields with solar panels and wind turbines now," says Kate. "Let's talk about solar panels another day," suggests mum. "Solar farms are used to produce non-fossil energy. Today we will talk about cows."

Mum remarks, "*There are less fields of cows nowadays because we are all trying to eat less red meat like beef which comes from cows.*"

"Really?" asks Tom. *"Yes,"* replies mum. *"Meat products like beef have a larger carbon footprint than vegetables. This is because the conversion of plant energy to animal energy is inefficient. Cows use up a lot of carbon energy eating grass to grow and make food in their bodies, which we eat as beef. Also they pass a carbon gas called methane from their backsides and they burp or belch a lot of methane. Methane is not good for the air as it traps heat from the sun and heats up the air much more than carbon dioxide. This is causing climate change."*

Mum continues, "*Methane is also released from natural systems such as freshwater systems. Here microorganisms act on organic matter in lakes, swamps and marshes to release methane. The release of methane from these will increase as the temperature rises. A source of man-made methane is the global oil and gas industry. Methane is called a greenhouse gas and it is one we need to reduce to save the planet.*"

"*Too much red meat is also not good for a healthy diet. To have a healthy diet we need to eat lots of fresh vegetables, as well as protein like beef or chicken. But some adults prefer plant based protein not animal protein, as plant protein production causes less carbon pollution. Further, it does not involve us rearing live animals just for humans to eat.*"

Finally, the children reach the end of the train journey. Their grandparents are there to meet them at the station and take their cases. Kate shows her grandmother the picture of wind turbines she has drawn on the journey. She will tell her grandparents about renewable wind energy. Tom will describe how they travelled on an electric train which was not powered by coal, a fossil fuel, but by wind generated energy.

Tom and Kate are pleased to arrive at their destination to spend a few days at the seaside with their grandparents.

What did we learn today? (tick the box if you understood and agree)

☐ Wind turbines use energy from the wind and convert it into electricity which is sent to the electricity power station.

☐ Cows need to eat a lot of grass for growth and their guts produce toxic methane which is released into the air.

☐ Some people prefer to eat plant protein rather than animal protein such as beef, chicken and pork.

☐ Methane is a strong greenhouse gas. It traps much more sunlight than carbon dioxide does and it heats up the air around our earth much more causing it to become hotter. This disturbs the normal climate balance.

☐ Animals and plants live together in conditions that are good for their health and growth and excess heat and temperature changes can become harmful to their survival.

Find out about Kate and Tom's Picnic at the Seaside on holiday in book 9.

Children Saving our Planet Series

Books

1. **Tom and Kate Go to Westminster**

2. **Kate and Tom Learn About Fossil Fuels**

3. **Tom and Kate Chose Green Carbon**

4. **Tress and Deforestation**

5. **Our Neighbourhood Houses**

6. **Our Neighbourhood Roads**

7. **Shopping at the Farm Shop**

8. **Travelling to a Holiday by the Sea**

9. **Picnic at the Seaside on Holiday**

10. **The Oceans and Coral**

11. **Our Carbon Footprint**

12. **Fire Fire**

13. **The Antarctic Warms Up**

14. **The Canada Catastrophe**

15. **The Coronavirus and saving the Planet**

16. **The Children's Rebellion and Climate Change**

These series of simple books explain the landmark importance of Children's participation in the Extinction rebellion protest. Children actively want to encourage and support adults to urgently tackle both the Climate and the Biodiversity emergencies. The booklets enable children at an early age to understand some of the scientific principles that are affecting the destruction of the planet. If global political and economic systems fail to address the climate emergency, the responsibility will rest upon children to save the Planet for themselves.

This series is dedicated to

Theodore, Aria and Ophelia.

Printed in the United States
by Baker & Taylor Publisher Services